I'M THIRSTY

LORRAINE JONES-WHITFIELD

ISBN: 9798218384746 (Paperback)
ISBN: 9798218398705 (e-Book)

DEDICATION

I dedicate this book to my parents, Lawrence, and Gladys Jones, whom God blessed to give me life on November 24, 1959. This is where my journey started.

I also dedicate this book to my husband for being my strength as I went through many storms and shed many tears. Thank you for having my back through thick and thin. I give all praises to God. Thank you for being my pastor, friend, husband, and the father of our children. Thank you, my love, for forty-plus years. I'm grateful for our God union.

To my one and only daughter, Keisha Sherrell, who's been a big inspiration. This book, *I'm Thirsty,* is a way to say thanks for not giving up despite life being tough. I've watched you push through pain, heartache, and even brokenness, but you've conquered what tried to bring you down.

Lastly, I'd like to dedicate this book to all the ladies in my women's ministry. "She Speaks Life Women's Bible

Study" And She Soars LLC, Mentoring, Coaching, and Counseling.

Isaiah 43:2 (KJV) *When thou pass through the waters, I will be with thee; and through the rivers, they shall not overflow thee: when thou walk through the fire, thou shalt not be burned; neither shall the flame kindle upon thee.*

God has proven to be that deliverer.

ACKNOWLEDGMENTS

Many other women led me along the way, prayed, and nurtured me as I grew into this dynamic woman of God. I say this because I was a broken young lady, and it took many women in my life to speak into my spirit. When they spoke the words 'Woman thou art Loosed', it spoke to the pain, purpose, and calling of a broken little girl inside of a woman's body.

Thank you, Joan Montgomery, for the Friday nights we spent together talking and praising the Lord as your beautician.

Thank you, Linda Mallory, for always encouraging me to continue my education.

Thank you, Grandmother Pauline, for being a powerful influence in my life. Your life led me to the Lord and living in your pain showed me that God was greater than any pain I could ever experience.

Thank you, Joan (Mrs. Montgomery). We laughed, cried, prayed, and believed that God gave us both the victory. We spent a lot of time together and when I felt that no one else believed in me, you did.

There are so many more women like Queenie Davis, who coached me into being a first lady to my pastor husband. She led by example and always had a smile despite her storms. She never talked about her storms, but we all have them. Her light was bright, and I witnessed God's love in her like the strong rays of the morning sun. She has blessed my life.

TABLE OF CONTENTS

INTRODUCTION

When we think of the women of the Bible, our minds go directly to women like Eve, Sarah, Miriam, Esther, Ruth, Delilah, Deborah, the woman with the issue of blood, and Mary (Jesus' mother). But there are many others in the bible that have a small appearance, and to some, their role was not important. As women today, we each have a vital role to play in our Christian journeys, which may lead to one or more life experiences similar to the Women in the Bible. Even if we don't see it, reading their stories will show us where we fit in and how many of them won their battles. What a blessing it is to see how they rose and began anew.

Biblical women were typically strong and self-sufficient, not depending on others. They feared the Lord and lived faithfully for Him because He empowered them to follow what He called them to do. It was through their actions that God inspired and taught us, and in fact, many of their problems had been with them since birth.

Many of us are fighting an inner war and our struggles have affected many aspects of our lives. These struggles or infirmities, as the Bible calls them, attach to us mentally, physically, and emotionally. As you continue to read, many of these women have problems stemming from birth and generational curses and could not break free. Today, many women stem from deep hurts, like the pain from rape, abuse, and addictions that are normally caused by unhealthy relationships. Some struggle with depression, anxiety, bullying, and Post-traumatic Stress Disorder (PTSD). Some are still trying to break free from the past.

It is important to remember that hiding things won't lead to proper healing and eventually, someone or something will expose them. God can uncover the wounds of any situation and He is the only one that can pour healing over all your wounds. Regardless of where you hurt, take time to repent, let go, and uncover your wounds. Get in the presence of the Lord and let him heal everywhere you hurt.

Women are experiencing some of the toughest storms of their lives, just as they did in the Bible days. Some are in the pits of life and trying to find their way out, but without help. Emotional traumas, mental-emotional disorders, and physical ailments plague many people. But God can heal all these afflictions if we give them to him. He prescribes whatever you need in His word. In the beginning was the Word, and the Word was with God, and the Word was God *(John 1:1)*. If we want God in the middle of our situations, we must pray the Word and believe it.

In one case, a woman who had been suffering from an issue of blood for twelve years found healing simply by touching the hem of His garment. As Martha struggled with anxiety, she failed to remember what was essential. After eighteen years, she is still bent out of shape and cannot fix her situation. Many women, including myself, had tragic childhood memories. They had failed relationships, raped by family members, terrible memories, messed up choices, and poor decisions. Some continue to make poor decisions even today. The experiences I had during my childhood crippled me, as they did many other women, left me thirsty, and I could not find my way forward. During my childhood, I experienced bitterness and a great deal of pain, which God ultimately healed.

It was all in the woman's attitude in *Luke 13* that kept her bent out of shape like many people because of pain and trauma from poor relationships. Although those memories may never go away, God can heal the pain and grief caused by them. As long as we love God and love our enemy as well as ourselves, He can erase them, and you will live again. God will heal you in ways you can never imagine, just as He did for me. He will love you like no other because He loves me. The Lord will free you so you can reach out to others who are suffering, have issues, are struggling with addictions, or who, in any way, have encountered the storms of life.

In *Jeremiah 18, the Lord told him to* arise and go to the potter's house and hear his words. The pots in the potter's hands became marred and unsuitable for their original purpose, so he molded them into something different. He found the broken pieces beautiful. This is the picture of us in the hands of the Lord, who is our Master Potter. He renews and restores us back into the vessels that he can use when we are willing and receptive to His plan for us. He reshapes us for his purpose.

God wants us to be healed, to be set free and made whole. He wants us to heal and be delivered. Healing takes time, and in that time, miracles happen instantly, and God can do things suddenly and immediately. This is part of our mental, physical, and emotional journey. It's a process that we must go through with patience to experience the true healing that God has planned for us. He was wounded for our transgressions, bruised for our iniquities, and the chastisement of our peace was upon Him. By His stripes, we were healed *(Isaiah 53:5)*. God wants to put a desire in the spirit of broken women. Once you can break free from your past without looking back, you know God has given you the strength to move forward. Satan wants you to live in your yesterday. He's constantly trying to show you what you cannot do with your passion, identity, and calling. He wants to draw your attention to your past and keep you moving backward, but Jesus came that you might have life in Him and have it abundantly. *John 10:10*

This book will focus on various women from different backgrounds in the bible who are seeking something. It is as though they are thirsty for a new life, a new place, a new relationship, some healing, a little peace, a change of scenery, or a new beginning. There may be some that seem unable to be fixed because they are just too broken. In their minds, they feel life has dealt them a bad hand and they cannot rectify it or they are too old to start something new. We find these same thirsts in our own lives when we face brokenness.

Being hurt and feeling like an outcast and unloved are signs of being broken by relationships. As a result, we find ourselves bitter and in pain with our attitudes. Some may see us as outcasts with no hope.

It doesn't matter who has rejected you in the past; we know Jesus will never reject you. God wants strong soldiers in his army who have allowed him to heal their souls. His words are filled with promises for those who act on what He says to do, and who will believe and trust in him. Taking God's word and His promise into account should guide the right choices moving forward for every hurting woman.

"Be still and know that I am God," Psalms 46:10 (KJV).

When women have experienced so much pain, forgiveness is the one thing that prepares them for growth and healing. Forgiveness releases us from physical, mental, and emotional bondage and frees us to move forward. It also enables us to forget those things behind us and press forward to our goals. Forgiving and releasing anger towards someone who has hurt us can save us years of unnecessary suffering. In *Matthew 6:12,* Jesus taught us to ask God to forgive us of our sins. Forgiveness requires letting go of something rather than holding onto it. *Hebrews 12:1* says we must lay aside every weight and sin that easily beset us and to run the race with patience. Holding onto pain can cause physical, mental, and emotional issues. God did not create us to be a burden, but He invites us to let things go and cast our cares on Him *1 Peter 5:7.* God wants us to be free by letting go of anger, guilt, shame, and hurts so we can move forward and live our purpose. When God comes to heal, He will reach down and pick you up from where you are and sometimes, He will do it immediately.

Therefore, forgiveness is a choice we must make to heal. Unforgiveness keeps you tied to the pain and keeps you in bondage, while the other person is living freely. Unforgiveness keeps you from receiving all that God has for you. Stand against the enemy. The greater your commitment, the more the devil will harass you. Be strong and know that God will be with you every step of the way. Trust the process because God has you and will not leave nor forsake you. Let it go.

Breaking the Wounds of the Past – Your soul is weary; your pains may weigh you down, but it has not conquered you yet. It is time to exhale the heart-breaking trauma of your past and 'Break Free.' *John 8:36.*

Strongholds – Negative thinking patterns that attack the heart. They are beliefs, traditions, habits, and characteristics that one has lived with for years, not letting go.

Experiencing jealousy, envy, favoritism, and comparison to others was a pain I had endured for a long time. My childhood wounds shaped my thoughts and shaped my life. These wounds produced major strongholds in my life, and I was ineffective, with no direction but to suffer.

Uncover that Wound – A wound that is covered will not heal well and strongholds become hard to tear down. It takes spiritual forces to tear down strongholds in your mind and it requires the power of God. In *Ephesians 6:10-18,* we learn to put on the whole armor of God to tear down strongholds. We also learn in *Romans 12:2* to be transformed by the renewing of our minds and in *2Corinthians 10:3-5,* we learn to cast down imaginations and line up our thoughts with God's word.

This war is personal and rarely starts suddenly. It may have been going on for months, years, or even from birth. In *Luke 13,* this woman's pain bent her out of shape for eighteen years. Her crippled spirit, which has been disabling her, is wearing out her body. The condition became obvious in her physical body and affected her emotional and mental well-being. *Psalms 109:22 (NLT) – For I am needy, my heart is full of pain.*

Emotional wounds will negatively affect us no matter who you are, where you live, or your current occupation. Whether you are a Preacher, Teacher, Coach, Doctor, Lawyer, Dentist, Construction Worker, Husband, Wife, or Child, life will still be cruel, hurtful, and hard if emotional wounds are not healed. Did you know that words hurt us worse than physical abuse? Bruises on your body will eventually go away, but words that are tucked in your memory can easily trigger your pain. We may look good on the outside but broken into many pieces on the inside. Emotional wounds can cause trauma and physical problems, leaving you emotionally disabled. Relationships can become crutches for us, and we become dependent on them without even realizing it. This kind of infirmity can put a strain on a relationship or friendship. Like the woman at the well in *John Chapter 4,* found herself in many relationships but not finding what she needed. She was thirsty for a relationship and was looking in all the wrong places. Every man in her life may have been different, but the same. She would find something different in each, but the relationship would leave her the same way, empty, lost, and broken emotionally, but still thirsty. Understanding the distinction between sin, spiritual struggles, personal weaknesses, and mental illness can help us avoid unnecessary difficulties.

While churches openly discuss healing for certain issues, they may overlook topics such as sex, relationships, special needs, and mental illnesses. I needed deliverance from bitterness, pain, abuse, and struggles, and no one knew how to help me. I was told to pray and seek God for healing because you have the Holy Spirit. My bitterness caused me to have depression, to live in darkness, and to cry without reason. It challenged my mind and played on my thoughts, and I ate when I was not hungry. Despite having the Holy Spirit, I had a deep thirst for God. I was hurting, and no one knew how to handle it. The Pastors' wives would tell me to pray and do not allow the devil to take hold of me. *Keep praying,* they would say, and the more they would say it, the madder I became. They did not know or understand that I needed deliverance. I longed for someone to speak words of encouragement and assist me in my journey to freedom. Everything has a root from which it grew, and, in my case, I buried it deep in the soil of my childhood. The roots were getting deeper and stronger. I needed to ease the pain that was destroying me. I was bent over and stayed that way for many years. More years than I wanted to.

God delivered me through my husband, teaching us how to break free through the word. He taught "Avoiding Bitterness" and that is when I understood the scripture and my breakthrough became real. Deliverance was here. I cried in repentance, and I straightened up. I felt relief, but still had to confront the issue at hand with the person who caused all this pain.

Healing cannot come from a desperate person who is fumbling through many broken pages of her life trying to find relief. It has to come from the word of God. It was in

Mark 11:22-24, where I found I needed God to hear my prayers of healing and forgiveness. I wanted to break free from that hostage situation. If I held that person hostage, someone or something would hold me hostage as well. I was a prisoner in my mind. The emotional pain of someone broken is harder to bear than physical pain and can be worse sometimes. In *John 1:11,* we see where Jesus came to identify our pain because he can relate to our rejection. He came unto His own, and his own received him not. Part of healing from emotional pain is faithfully believing that God can heal you everywhere you hurt. He heals the brokenhearted and binds up their wounds *Psalms 147:3*. Following Jesus is the first step to emotional healing. He is One who restores our souls and leads us to the paths of healing *Psalms 23*. We must keep in mind that healing is a process. One where we must make good choices and stay away from negative interactions that will set us back from making wise and healthy choices. This type of emotional pain is like a bruise that slowly heals and can be re-injured again if you do not break free. The spirit is willing, but the flesh is weak. In the Spirit we take captive every thought to make it obedient to Christ. *2 Corinthians 10:5*. Following Jesus is the first step to emotional healing. He is One who restores our souls and leads us to the paths of healing. *(Psalms 23)*.

Recognizing that Spirit of Infirmity – Many things can endanger us, and that spirit of infirmity can come in many forms. Infirmity is physical or mental weakness. It bends you out of shape and cripples you. A broken spirit crushed by life's issues and difficulties resists. It can be a spiritual weakness and it can be so strong that it keeps you away from God.

Some people stay busy to avoid painful emotions. Some will even isolate themselves, intending to internalize the pain. If we are on this earth, we will experience pain, and it may be impossible to avoid. Some deny the pain, and many medicate their pain or project it onto someone else. The woman sought healing from many doctors, but none could help her. Then she heard about Jesus and pushed through the crowd to touch his garment.

Personal War – When we say personal, that means it was a war she struggled with all alone. It was an individual situation that only God could free her from. We must put perspective on our past and move forward. Healing something that is torn won't be that easy. Jesus will heal those broken hearts, and he heals a contrite spirit *Psalm 51:17.* So, spending quality time with God is a vital necessity. God can heal our brokenness. *Psalms 5:3 (NIV) – In the morning, Lord, you hear my voice; in the morning I lay my request before you and wait expectantly.* We must take uninterrupted and quality time with God, read the word, confess our sins, exalt Him in prayer, and meditate on His word. We are in spiritual warfare. A battle with the enemy who will never let up. The battlefield in your mind is your thoughts and we need to identify our infirmity and apply God's word to it. We must refuse to be anxious, angry, dissatisfied, envious, depressed, bitter, hopeless, and refuse to stay there. Negative emotions reveal doubt, and if we thoroughly trust God, why would we doubt him? Why are we bent out of shape and have these issues instead of seeking God? Why do we have issues, needy, and too busy for God? We are all born with an assignment, and it is time that we free ourselves from our past wounds. So, let us straighten up our life and walk in God's promises. His word heals and delivers and, most of all, it will set us free.

CHAPTER 1

EVE'S MESS

"Eve" means "life," but in the beginning, she was just called "woman." Yes, she started us all off in the beginning. She was Adams's gift, the first virgin, first woman in the garden, first mother, and the first to experience the first death and first deception. She was the mother of all living. The first being fashioned by the hand of God. She had everything all-natural and with no additives, the first home in the garden, first marriage, first sons and she grieved first. She came into a perfect world, with her husband and God. They were not a product of an evolutionary process nor an imagination of humanity but created by God. He created them in His image and in the image of God, He created him *Genesis 1:27.*

Eve was created from the rib of man. She was not created to walk behind him nor in front of him, but she was created to walk beside him, to love him, and to be a help mate for him. To meet his every need, naturally and spiritually, emotionally, and sexually. Adam said, "This is now bone of my bones and flesh of my flesh: she shall be called Woman because she was taken out of man *Genesis 2:23*. God had specifically created her to be a matching helper to her husband, Adam. She was created to be his companion. Her companionship was more than that of the animals and less than that of God. Adam had no problem relating to Eve because she was a part of him. Their roles were different, and their needs were also different, but they understood one another's roles.

When people come together in the Spirit, they too are picture-perfect characteristics of God. The enemy wants to declare war on marriages and cause separations or divorces. He knows if he can separate that bond, then he can destroy the home. The enemy knows that if he can tear down communication in the home and exploit their needs, he can destroy the total picture of godliness.

Understanding the right relationship between men and women requires us to let go of sinful and distorted thoughts about God's word. Men are good providers, while women are more agreeable and better at recognizing others' emotions, as men are more assertive. But a man needs respect, companionship, and a home that is free from the stresses of the world. So, ought men to love their wives as their bodies *Ephesians 5:28-32*? A woman needs love and meaningful opportunities and conversations. She needs someone to show her kindness, respect her privacy, hold her secrets, communicate with her, and love her like she wants to be loved.

A successful marriage requires adjusting, adapting, communicating, compromising, valuing, respecting, and accepting differences. Commitment is essential to a successful marriage. It is that covenantal bond that holds families together. The marriage covenant provides security, financial stability, and extended ties to family and children. This is an agreement between the husband and wife in all areas of their marriage.

Eve's Choice–Then one day Eve's world fell apart. Satan sought her out after she was created. He knew something about Eve and what she would do. He scoped her out as he does all women. The enemy is aware of their strengths and will relentlessly target them. In the evening's cool, he made his move.

And he said, 'Did God say which of the trees not to eat from? Did he say if you eat of it, you will surely die? *Genesis* 3. Eve took the time to converse with that evil thing. She knew what God said, but it was the lust of her eyes, lust of flesh, and pride of life and a doubt that made her disobey God's instruction and look the other way. Maybe if she would have communicated with her husband about what God had told them, but she felt like this would be the chance of a lifetime – more knowledge or power. Deception led her to lose everything later. Lifetime – more knowledge or power. The power of choice.

Inadequate communication is a major cause of divorce in marriages.

Just as soon as God created Eve and gave them careful instructions, the enemy sought her out, and that is how all the deception began. Lies were told and their house came falling apart.

The serpent appeared in the garden and tempted Eve, but she didn't seek God's guidance or strength to resist. He came to entice her and draw her away from godly principles. The enemy made her thirst after the carnal things in life. Satan's major goal is to erase the lines of distinction. He came to destroy the home, marriage, and family unit. He came to distract Eve and make her doubt God's word. Satan took control of that serpent and used it to work as the temptation to sin.

Sin had driven a wedge deep inside their hearts and they thirsted for things they knew nothing about. God issued a stern warning about the hardships in life, specifically mentioning hard labor for Eve and increased work for Adam. He would go back to the dust of the earth from which he was formed.

Tempted by Satan, he urged her to focus on the one thing she could not have. Eve lost sight of her blessings without gratitude. She did not know of shame, embarrassment, manipulation, envy, hurt, bitterness, grief, resentment, or guilt. They let the enemy's whisper influence them, leading to doubt and reasoning with God. The enemy tries to get us to focus on selfish fulfillment. Once we succumb to his captivating words, we're left with regret from the disappointing outcome. Guilt and shame produce sin.

We sometimes allow people to speak into our spirits, whether good or bad. We harken to it as Eve did the serpent. She was thirsty for wisdom, knowledge, and power simply when God told her "No." Against her better judgment, she listened to the enemy and entertained the thought in her mind. She began to waver in the spiritual walk with God. *James 1:6* – waver is to be tossed to and fro like the wind and when we waver, we walk in uncertainty as to hesitate or walk in disbelief. Eve fell prey to the strong whisper of Satan. Her eyes became illuminated as she witnessed God's intended vision, safeguarding her from sin. They were naked and did not feel ashamed.

After stealing from that tree of knowledge, Eve faced the consequences of her disobedience and punishment came to all three: Adam, Eve, and the serpent.

They lost their home in the garden and are now homeless and looking for a new home. Eve did this with her reckless thoughts and ideas. She learned from a painful experience that disobedience will cost you everything. If only she had talked to God instead of doing things her way, things could have been different.

She lost a great deal, and now her children will bear the resemblance of sin. So, after the garden, Adam and Eve started a family and gave birth to Cain and Abel. She knew these were her miracles and, once again, she was happy.

The spirit of disobedience was hanging around that family again. Later, Cain would kill Abel because of jealousy and fierce anger because God chose not to accept his sacrifice. So, you see, disobedience caused murder and separation. Eve lost two sons all at once. She lost one to death and the other to the curse of God. I cannot imagine grief like that, but it happens. The wife was in pain, grieving, and hurting as the husband worked and sweated. I remember when my mother-in-law lost two sons back-to-back. Both to cancer and I could not imagine a mother's pain like that, but I could feel her pain and grief because before that she already lost a son, daughter, and husband. She held on to God and prayed through the pain.

Eve would bury one and never see the other again. She never mentioned seeing him again, so he was dead in her eyes. He left and turned his back on God. Many children leave home and lose their connection to their parents and God.

Grief and trauma come to us all, and life seems so hard when we lose a loved one. Many of us face financial struggles, disasters, and broken relationships. Life's unfairness piles up and we feel as if we cannot make it another day. God gives us strength to persevere and peace that surpasses all understanding.

Her mind became unsettled after talking to darkness, even though God's words were clear. She faced the consequences of her actions, as Satan's deception destroyed her, both spiritually and physically. *John 10:10 - Satan comes to kill, steal, and destroy.* Some women face low self-esteem without realizing they are victims of their emotional strongholds. We must give God all our secrets and sacrifices to allow the power of the anointing to touch our lives in all our broken areas. He will take our secrets and ease our pain, then touch every area where we are hurting. Even though I ran like Cain, I know he did that for me. My grandma's death compelled me to run away from the problems and pain of my childhood. All I knew was I had to escape, even if it meant leaving my child behind. It was a stronghold that I had no power to break. The hurt and the pain from the people in my life telling me I would be nothing and I was just nobody in life all took a toll on me.

Pain and grief will make you do things that are not normal. My grandma died when I was 21 and it was like my world ended. It hurt, and I did not know how to deal with it. So, I was in my place wandering around looking for love, drugs, and trying to ease that pain. I was running away from home and not knowing where I was going. There are many

Cains wandering in a lost world called nowhere, thinking they are living but in pain. Running from hurt, anger, disappointment, envy, comparison, and rejection. I kept running and continued to be broken.

Sometimes as women, we make wrong choices, and listen to the wrong gossip, and have the wrong thoughts in our minds. Those mind-binding spirits are real. You are thrown around and jerked in different directions until you suddenly fall and can't escape. The world transformed into a captivating place, yet love was nowhere to be found; now I understand it was lust, not love. The moment of indulgence can bring enjoyment, but it's only a temporary fix. The results of sin will bring devastating results and bitter regret.

Through lies and deception, Satan comes to alter your destiny. God has the power to restore you, allowing His Spirit to fill you with wholeness. He can restore all who come to him in humility and repentance. Confessing our sins is necessary, and He will forgive them. The choice is ours: follow God, walk in the light, and leave darkness behind.

CHAPTER 2

WHO IS LEAH?

She was thirsty. Thirsty for love, but in all the wrong places. Have you ever searched for love in all the wrong places and convinced yourself that he was the one? Well, that is Leah's story. In *Genesis 29,* we find Leah being Laban's oldest daughter and the one that was made fun of because of her looks, being compared to her younger sister Rachel. Rachel's beauty and vanity made her highly desirable to men, while Leah was the subject of mockery.

Can you imagine being single, crossed-eyed, unwanted, and wounded? Her heart ached with pain, and it was evident on her face.

After deceiving his father and stealing his brother's birthright, Jacob finds himself at Uncle Laban's house in Harran. There Jacob fell in love with the younger sister Rachel. These were his first cousins. His mother's brothers' children.

Leah, being the eldest, should have been the first to wed. However, because of her crossed eyes and lack of beauty compared to Rachel, she was unloved and hated. Everyone overlooked her and always compared her to Rachel. Can you imagine how Leah felt? Does this story sound like your story? It's extremely similar to mine. Hearing that you're unwanted and ugly, with no potential for success, made me believe I would be a loser. Words can cause harm, leave bruises, and inflict pain, and anyone who depicts this behavior is cruel and filled with hate.

Jacob made a deal with Laban to work seven years for Rachel's hand in marriage. Those seven years passed by fast, and it was time to marry the little beauty. Laban threw a big party but, instead of giving him Rachel, he tricked him that night and gave him Leah. Blinded by love, Jacob did not notice at first this was not Rachel until he looked into her eyes, and he knew then. Jacob felt ripped off, betrayed, and hurt by the deception. But remember earlier he did the same thing to his brother Esau by stealing his birthright and then running for his life. It seems that the family has a tendency towards deception and trickery. Jacob experienced the consequences of the generational curse, and it was unpleasant. Viewing things from a different angle, I could understand Leah's feelings. The depth of her hurt and pain must have been even greater, making it extremely cruel to set her up like this. She already felt rejected, while they always praised Rachel.

Meanwhile, Leah was married to a man who did not love her. She experienced hurt, pain, hatred, and rejection in her marriage. Another woman, her sister Rachel, captivated Jacob. Being married to two sisters at one time conflicted with God's plan for marriage. God's plan was for one man and one woman. But they did it in disobedience, anyway. This was just continued pain and brought on hatred and bitterness.

Laban caused the drama and didn't feel sorry for his deceit. He justified it by saying it was tradition to marry off the older daughter first, knowing that no one wanted her. Sadly, Jacob was obviously in love with Rachel and not Leah. But because of the hatred they had for Leah, the Lord allowed her to conceive *Genesis 29:31*. Through the rejection, jealousy, pain, hurt, and rejection, God still blessed her. Leah grew up with hurt and pain and always had to walk behind everyone like she did not belong to the family. She stood out because of her unique attitude and appearance. People have a tendency to judge others solely by their outward appearance, ignoring the true nature within.

Because of this situation, Leah was fortunate enough to become pregnant and have her first child. Leah names him Ruben, having witnessed my suffering. Following that, she had additional sons and a jealous sister. Rachel's jealousy toward her sister led to intense hatred. God withheld His blessing and closed her womb because of her attitude and hatred. The tight closure left her with no options except to converse with God. She was empty, thirsty, bitter, and filled with intense anger. Her anger was so intense that she developed a strong hatred for her sister. Can you imagine being hated by your sibling and tossed to the side? Or feeling unwanted, ugly, and worthless. That is Leah's story, my story, and our pain.

There was a call in the spirit for women like Leah. God is calling those who are hurting and thirsty for something better. *Matthew 5:6 (KJV) Blessed are they which do hunger and thirst after righteousness for they shall be filled.*

Leah thought he would love her if she had his son. Jacob only loved what she could give him (sons) and what Rachel could not. God has seen her bent over, thirsty, hated and he saw the hurt but, God loved her with an everlasting love. Despite her husband and sister treating her badly, Leah endured. God blessed her with motherhood, giving her four sons, but no more for Jacob. Leah's children, including her fourth son Judah, received God's blessing and became the ancestor of Jesus Christ and the tribe of Judah.

Faith Moves–Broken and dysfunctional homes sometimes produce broken children, and it is the children that are caught up in the hurts of the parents. But we must allow God to heal and adjust those damaged places and the hurts of our past. Leah loved Jacob, but she knew he did not belong to her, neither did his heart.

In Leah's hurts, God held her in His loving arms on those quiet and lonely nights when no one was around. He touched her with his sensitive hands and blessed her with His empathetic heart. When Leah let go and gave it to God, he quenched her thirst from the pains of her past and the pains of an unwanted marriage. She realized that regardless of how people hurt her, God would ultimately turn things around. God desires to restore broken women and reignite their desire to walk in their destiny. But there will not be any desire until they have a genuine relationship with him.

At sixteen, I was pregnant, broken, and wandering around, not knowing God. Thrown into the pit by many and feeling unloved. The pain of what some would call a mistake was unbearable, but I refused to give up my child. Like Leah, the pain was obvious, and being alone was real.

Regardless of my situation, I called out to God and, despite my lack of familiarity with him, he listened to me. There have been many occasions in my life where I've made mistakes, yet He still chose me *John 15:16* and had knowledge of me since I was in my mother's womb. I didn't let my past or background prevent me from moving forward. I had to fight through the pain and discover a new path for myself. Suffering led to more suffering and the tears never stopped. I was trapped in anger and bitterness, desperately searching for a way to let go. Just like Leah, I also had a child named Judah (Praise) and she praised God despite her pain. She realized it was time to move ahead, and I felt the same. God was preparing her for His plan and purpose, so she could live out her calling. Anything is possible for those who believe.

> *Lord, I thank you for healing and deliverance. As a woman, I, like Leah, feel hurt, unwanted, and rejected. I plead for release from the pain I've carried for so long. Lord, release me from the thoughts of fear, bondage, insecurity, guilt, shame, and condemnation. Grant me strength and courage to meditate on your word day and night, so that I may achieve the success you have planned for me.*
>
> *I declare and decree that I can do all things through Christ who strengthens me (Philippians 4:13). My goal is to see the purpose in your plan for me when reflecting on my past, not let childhood pains consume me, and draw my strength from the Joy of the Lord.*
>
> *In Jesus Name, Amen.*

CHAPTER 3

SARAH'S BIG MESS

Neither gives place to the devil–Ephesians 4:27(KJV)

Do not allow Satan to plug into you and destroy you through clever seductions. For Eve, all it took was one whisper in her ear. It took one thought to change her entire world. She got caught up in the moment and did it without discernment. It is not enough to reject the enemy's schemes; you must focus on the plans and promises of God.

God summoned Abraham to a foreign land, but he brought his nephew Lot despite being told not to. This is how life was in the Military for my family. Every time my husband got orders, it was time to uproot and leave to go to another state or country. Packing up and leaving friends and family behind and away we go. I did not question it, but I made a vow and I had to leave and cleave unto my husband. It was not so bad, but it was lonely. So, after a while, we wanted a baby. Just like Sarah, I could not conceive for a little while, and that was hard and devastating to me. I kept praying and trusting in God that one day in his time, it would happen.

Well, Sarah's hopes faded as she thought she could not bear Abraham a son. She forgot all about God's promise and her barrenness caused her to produce a plan of her own.

Sarah was thirsty, and I mean thirsty. She wanted a child by any means necessary. Sarah's hopes of bearing Abraham a son faded. She was hurting, and she was desperate. She gave her Egyptian handmaid to her husband to produce a child. This was not pleasing to God, but Sarah pushed on with her scheme.

Her handmaid became her surrogate mother. She would carry the baby for her and give her husband that baby as promised. What woman in their right mind would give their husband to another woman to marry? Being a man, Abraham did not back down. He went along with Sarah's mess and took advantage of that opportunity. Her fear, doubt, and thirst set her in motion. Sarah's faith faltered because she wanted to assist God in fulfilling his promise.

Life is not Always Fair – She knew it would work. But soon after conception, these two ladies despised one another. They spoke evil to one another. Females are envious. Evil speaking refers to slanderous, abusive, or blasphemous speech. We allow our tongues to get hideous and out of control. When someone speaks evil to another person, it can cause significant harm. Sarah caused Hagar and Abraham's relationship to begin, but later struggled with it when she became pregnant. She caused Hagar so much pain that she fled into the wilderness. She was pregnant, hurt, and alone. Hagar would return to Sarah out of obedience to God. Our attitudes can sometimes hinder the fulfillment of our promise, so it is necessary to go back and make things right. God has a way of humbling us.

The Lord told Abraham that his heir would not be Sarah's child, but a son from his own body. The Lord asked Abraham to look at the stars and said that his descendants would be as many as them. I often wonder if Sarah heard the promise, or did Abraham forget to tell her what God had said to him?

Well, her fear, doubt, and thirst for that child took over, and the plan was set in motion. She faltered in her faith, and all she knew was that she wanted that promise. Unlike myself, I went from doctor to doctor on the Military Base and they had no answers. They gave me a thermometer, and I bought a pregnancy test and every time we tried, we both got disappointed. I would break the thermometer and the pregnancy test would say negative. I feel you, Sarah, but I never thought of giving my husband to another woman. It took faith in God to turn it all around. It would only cause problems, and I would be despised like Sarah was by Hagar. Yes, Hagar slept with Abraham, and she conceived right away. She was pregnant and trouble started immediately. Now, Hagar is the mother and Sarah is the stepmom. How twisted can a situation get? I tell you when you do not follow God's plan, it will be a mess. She had no intention of giving her baby away. Hagar was charged with treating Sarah in a harsh and disrespectful manner. Can you believe it?

The situation was dreadful. When we step out of God's will and do things on our own, we do not expect a great outcome *Proverbs 3:5-6.*

TIME OF EXPECTANCY – While waiting on your dream or promise, sometimes you just must wait. In waiting, you cannot be in despair but be expecting your promise. Sarah felt there was no hope. She thought she was getting too old, and time was running out. But it is that appointed time we must keep in mind. Nothing is impossible with God.

By the time I turned 60, I had achieved my master's degree and started writing my vision. I was determined to give birth to my dreams and plans. We must learn how to rest in the Lord and trust Him in our process. I am still giving birth to my dreams and setting goals for a greater outcome *Psalms 37:7.* Do not worry about the Hagars and move forth in your dream. God has given all of us that child of promise. We all have an Isaac inside of us, and we don't have to settle for an Ishmael, even though the promise entitled him. So, wait and enjoy the pregnancy.

I waited on the birth of my vision and, like Sarah, I had to wait on the birth of my son after many times trying to conceive. It is all in His plan. We just must wait on the Lord and allow Him to renew our strength. Isaiah 40:31. God wants us to focus on walking by faith and not lose sight of our vision, just like Sarah and Hagar did. The thing we must do is to be obedient to God and take it step by step. Your vision will happen as God moves in your life because He is always behind the scenes, pulling things together and making it all fit into place. We must focus on that vision and not give up. It will happen. We must wait for our vision and expect God to move as he says he will. Sometimes we need patience and perseverance.

Habakkuk speaks of the vision that will be fulfilled at the appointed time, and those who are patient will be rewarded. In the end, the vision will speak and not deceive. So, expect to give birth but go through the process. Sarah's dream seemed slow. She laughed, and her laughter turned into trust. She trusted God. I wonder if she trusted him at the first movement of her baby. Did she trust him during morning sickness? I know I went through changes trying to have my third child, and I did not even know that I was pregnant with him. All things worked together for the good of those who love the Lord and are called according to His purpose, so my prayers were answered and happened at God's appointed time. Hold on because there is a purpose for everything. Keep faithing it.

CHAPTER 4

YOUR FAITH WILL CHANGE YOUR SITUATION

Psalms 5:3- In the morning you hear my voice O Lord: In the morning I prepare for you and watch and wait.

B***ENT OUT OF SHAPE***–The woman in *Luke 13* was suffering because of something that attacked her 18 years earlier. Her battle did not just start, but it was a personal war going on in her body. This thirst has been deeply rooted in her past and the prescription she needed was in the word of God. Once you recognize your infirmity, recognize your enemy, and identify the tactics, then you can move on to your prescription. Until you diagnose the problem, you will not know how to treat it. In coaching and counseling, we must learn how to listen and hear what the client is saying. We need to be present for them. Here, the situation attacked her, and it was deep within her for

18 years. It caused her to be physically bent over. She was crippled, and it was not just physical but it touched her in all areas of her life. Lifting herself was impossible because of the pain, even her attitude had her bent out of shape, and she was thirsty. She was in search of her identity, her way in life, and needed a miracle; she needed to break free. But did not know how.

Many people go through traumatic situations, and that was her problem. The word trauma means "wound," so trauma is a wound to the mind, heart, and soul of a person. Many women go through all kinds of trauma, like sexual abuse, rape, domestic violence, abuse, grief, and war. Some are silent about what they have endured, and some are sitting on the pews at church right beside you. They are in pain, twisted over, and come for relief, but no one recognizes it. Some people have tried to share their experiences, but others do not believe them which causes them to become withdrawn and unsure of whom to trust or what to do. So she goes within, dealing with an internal personal war that is affecting her deeply.

This type of wounding happens when suffering overwhelms what we consider normal human coping. Memories of trauma affect the person's sleep, destroy relationships, and capacity to work and torment one's emotions. Mental, emotional, and spiritual wounds, like physical ones, can fester up if not properly cared for. That is why it is important to understand a person's struggles and not try to silence them or treat them as if they do not have faith. It is important to remember that God will never leave you nor forsake you whenever you are discouraged by circumstances faced in life. Tough times may come to most people, but God will bring you through. God's definition of evil, often not discussed in churches, is assumed by many to exclude sexual abuse, rape, and domestic violence. We come to church bent over and leave the same way. It is imperative that we listen and do not silence the victims of trauma and give them a voice and listen to their pain, anguish, and turmoil. This woman may have experienced trauma and abuse, which caused her to feel vulnerable and violated. Her childhood could have been violated, her marriage could have been broken, she may have experienced rejection and abuse, and her children could have been dealing with drug addiction. It could have been many things, but it was her choice to give her problems, pain, and past hurts to God. It seems the older we get; we feel as if it is hard for our situation to change. Some may feel there is no hope, or we are just too old. We may feel change is too late.

Whenever I think of the issues of these women in the Bible, I am reminded of my pain. It reminded me of the rejection, hurt, and abuse I endured as a child. The memories of my childhood haunted me for most of my young and adult life. They crippled me mentally, physically, and emotionally and it was like that pain would never end. I was not only bitter but hurt, angry, had lots of resentment, and was in bondage to someone's abuse and strong harsh words that stayed with me. This pain would not leave me, no matter how hard I would try. It felt like torment and therefore I was thirsty for something new and a release from that pain. It was a torment, and the pain was nasty. Suffering from mental brokenness. I did not know how to allow the Lord into my broken mess. But he was always nearby.

At sixteen, I was pregnant, and for seven months, no one knew it. Single, in school, and living at home with my parents waiting for a baby to be born. After the secret was out, the abuse started. I was beaten, slapped, and pushed on the kitchen floor of that farmhouse where we lived. I experienced pain, devastation, and an unquenchable thirst for love that was never fulfilled. I was numb and did not know what to do but endure it all. It bent me out of shape, my attitude was wrong, my heart was bitter and empty. I was like this woman of eighteen years but could relate to Leah as well. I felt unwanted, unloved, and always knew that I was not pretty because they would validate that daily. "You are ugly, mean, and you won't get anywhere in life." The tears, the pain, and the hurt I had to endure. The situation left me feeling broken, angry, and bitter. The pain never stopped. I went from hurt to anger, resentment, and bitterness; they all kept me bent out of shape. I was thirsty and in need of a way out.

Despite all that, I gave birth to my son and graduated from High School, thanks to my aunt. I continued my journey as

I worked at MacDonald's on the weekends to take care of my child. My struggle was real, and it hurt me. I was tired, bitter, but had to keep pushing. By then, my attitude was worse, and it bent me out of shape. My emotions were all over the place, but this was my life and I had to make it happen. Although our challenges may differ, we all struggle. My struggle is not yours. Just as Jesus came to save the lost, he did not come to judge, so please do not judge me either.

Jesus saw a hurting person, and he ministered to their need. He surrounded himself with broken, bleeding, hurtful, thirsty people. His actions differed from ours. He called out to the woman who was broken, hurting, and crippled *Luke 13:11-13*. For years, she came to church on Sundays, always sitting in the same pew. For years, I did the same thing, with no one realizing how broken I was. Then, one day during a Bible Study, Jesus met me and other women who were also broken.

BROKEN INTO PIECES–He will restore to you what the cankerworm and locust ate up *Joel 2:25*. The enemy wanted to change my destiny. God needed to heal my pain. I needed restoration but did not know how to get it. In order to enter the life of someone who has been reduced, limited, and altered by suffering, we must reduce ourselves as well. Those who are hurting have suffered trauma, fewer words, quiet voices, patience, and pause so that they do not feel so overwhelmed. The church should emulate Jesus and provide assistance, companionship, and comfort to those who are suffering. Just like the night at the bible study and Pastor Whitfield taught on Overcoming Bitterness, it hit the hearts of all three of us women. It touched the part of our lives that had us bent over. It pierced our hearts into repentance. We were hurting and I the more. Just know that it is important to understand that these struggles did not silence me, nor did the Pastor treat us as a failure of faith. The pain and suffering I endured broke down my walls, overran my orders, and violated my boundaries. I needed that compassionate care and deliverance as that woman did. Jesus saw her need and showed her compassion as he called her to him. He understood the pain and struggles she experienced. He summoned her and spoke the words, "Woman, Thou Art Loosed." He acknowledged her suffering and freed her from it, beckoning her to the forefront. He spoke to her heart, pain, abuse, and bitterness, and offered a healing word.

God needed to deliver me and to heal my pain. I needed restoration but did not know how to get it. Being always told you will be nobody or nothing! You are hateful and will get nowhere. Leah's pain was like mine, as I stated. It hurts when it comes from family and speaking that negatively into your spirit. Unlike Leah, who kept having children with a man who didn't love her, I had a miscarriage with my second child and didn't have any more kids until I got married. God knows all, and as I continued to push through the pain and my struggles, I realized I needed to be free. I did not know God as I know Him now and being unloved and hurt, I became defensive. I tried to numb the pain by partying, drinking, smoking, and getting high, but it only worsened, and I knew I had to make a change.

FORGETTING THOSE THINGS THAT ARE BEHIND – At 21, I got married. The party slowed down, but the drugs did not. A military spouse and broken again. I may not have a baby in my womb, but I'm still a Mom with a four-year-old child and a Mom who has custody. The birth of a child is one of God's greatest blessings. Children are a heritage of the Lord, and the fruit of the womb is his reward *Psalms 127:3-5*. Broken homes sometimes produce broken children. My parents raised my son well. Although it was painful, I had faith that he would eventually understand my story and that God would take care of him. It was my pain because it hurt to leave my son behind, but God planned it to be that way. God had a promise and at the time I did not understand the plan and I only saw the pain.

Many people read children as living epistles. Parenting involved responsibility and they did not believe that my husband and I could do this, but we never had the opportunity.

Yes, I wanted the best for him and my family. I prayed nightly for God's will for safety for him as he grew up. Yes, I hurt being without him all my life and the pain did not get easier. There I go again. I had to deal with that unforgiveness and bitterness; I had a hurt that only Jesus could heal. Freedom was what I needed. My husband loved me, but I still felt broken, and now I had the added pain of a missing piece. I was still depressed. I was in darkness and pain and empty. It was as if someone took my baby directly out of my womb. Again, the things covered do not heal well. Tired of being chained to my past and all this hurt, I did not know how to release it, but I knew I needed to. Like Leah, the woman bent over, all I wanted was to be loved. I desired the love from my family. I know they loved me, but strangely. No matter how tough life may seem, people with a past need to make their way to Jesus. Regardless of the obstacles within and without, we must reach out to Him. God knows your history and therefore you do not have to tell everyone your pain. He will turn your pain into purpose. He makes it into something marvelous. *Psalms 139:14*.

Jesus touched the woman with infirmity after he called her to him. When Jesus calls, be receptive to His touch. If you can't receive from Him, you may end up like the woman at the well, in need of a relationship, intimacy, or simply thirsty. Like the woman bent over, he knew her, and he touched and healed her. He chose me too *John 15:16*. He touches us in the world and heals us from this pain. We may seek help by going from one person to another, but Jesus is the only answer. If you have enough force to bend yourself over and become thirsty, then you must find Jesus to straighten yourself back up. To break free from that infirmity – I need to recognize the influences it has on my body.

Both she and I knew that it would take some time before she could rebuild her life. It was 18 long years for me before I could share with my son "because" he was living there and not with us. I had many things to overcome, and I allowed this to handicap me for many years. I dealt with confidence and insecurities and so much hurt. It was one day in February God called to me and I obeyed his call. It beat me up. Still broken, he continued to call me over to him one Sunday in Augusta, Georgia, at a small church on base. He was aware of what happened to me at sixteen and he remains knowledgeable about it today. That day, he saved me from so much and I experienced joy unlike any other. He knew I needed a release and to be renewed, and he was ready to reveal to me the reason I went through all this mess. The healing process began, and God straightened up my life. He promised me that, as a broken woman and like the others, we would recover everything that had been stolen from us, rebuild our self-esteem, regain our confidence, and restore our integrity and self-respect. This is due to us. So, you see, we do not have to be bent over anymore. The power of the anointing has set us free, and the joy of the Lord is our strength. I may not change where I have been, but I am certainly going to change where I am going. When we spend time with God, He has a way of transforming us. Changing our hearts and minds. He has a way of healing us everywhere we hurt. He transforms us to be more like Him.

CHAPTER 5

HAGAR

His Mistress and His Mistake Genesis 16.

We live in a world where sin is commonplace and excessive and society is all confused and mixed up. Hagar was a foreigner and an Egyptian slave. Single, lonely woman and she had limited resources because she was a slave. She took on the responsibility of being Sarah's handmaiden. Abraham and she became lovers because of Sarah's plan. Hatred, manipulation, and mistreatment were inflicted upon her. She was treated like a piece of property as if she had no value. She was a part of Sarah's scheme to give birth to a child.

Psalms 127:3-5 (KJV) Lo Children are a heritage of the Lord, and the fruit of the womb is his reward. As arrows are in the hand of the mighty man; so are the children of the youth. Happy is the man who has his quiver full of them;

they shall not be ashamed, but they shall speak with the enemies in the gate.

Children are living epistles and are a blessing of the Lord. Being a Mom of seven children is a blessing and raising five of them was sometimes a challenge – it did not come with a manual, but it was by trial and error. Psalms relate children to arrows. Can you imagine a broken arrow? Think about the children who have been abused or are homeless without guidance. Some have been abused at the hands of a broken adult. Some people call these children abused kids or children who are victimized in this world. But these children are broken arrows. Broken because of another broken life.

Hagar Thrown out – Hagar was thrown out of the camp. Sarah created this drama and now she despises Hagar. (Genesis 16:4). Sarah inflicts her and Hagar runs away into the wilderness. She got far before she heard a voice speaking out to her. The voice spoke and told her you have a son, and you are to name him Ishmael (meaning God heard your misery) and the promise is unto you as well.

Alone, a single Mom with nothing. Eventually, she returns but at the direction of God. Hagar did not argue, but she followed the instructions and returned to Sarah and Abraham. God saw her misery, her hurts, her anxiety and bitterness about the future and he knew about it all. Just like many women, Hagar finds herself back in the wilderness.

This time it was by force rather than by choice. Here it is sixteen years later, and she is still struggling because Sarah dismissed Hagar and Ishmael from their home. Can you imagine being a single Mom with nowhere to go? The only thing you have is a son and a promise. But her focus was not on the promise, but on finding a place to live. Homeless and a single Mom. No money and hurt, filled with bitterness. She humbly left not knowing where her next meal would come from and no family to help her. It is the children that get caught up in the drama and the crossfire of angry parents and suffer in the end.

As a foster Mom, I see children who are broken and struggling with separation anxiety, unable to understand why their parents didn't want them. There was a lack of understanding regarding the troubled past of these parents, which involved abuse, sexual abuse, and drug addiction. They were running into their wilderness, as Hagar did. They were unaware of their identity and had no sense of direction. Hagar entered the wilderness of Beersheba with Ishmael, feeling bewildered and with no companions. Abraham provided Hagar's son with bread and a water bottle when their supplies were depleted. As soon as all the water was gone, she placed Ishmael under the shrubs and distanced herself from him because it would be too painful to watch him die. As she was by the fountain of Shur, she was given a promise. Because the Lord has seen your affliction, I will multiply your seed abundantly. God's provision never ceases, even in the face of adversity. God is always faithful to his promises. Our heartache and cries are seen and heard by God, so there's no need to be anxious because of the existence of evildoers; we simply have to believe in his word. The Lord supplies provision before we even see the need. Hagar sat down and thought this was the end, but God never forgot His promise to her. He supplied and brought healing to Hagar and her son. God truly hears the cry of the afflicted (Job 34:28).

HAGAR'S EYES OPENED – Sometimes our blessings are right in front of us. It is sometimes beyond where we are looking. Because of our disappointments, our vision can be clouded and that may be why some of us cannot find our purpose. We allow those painful places of our past to hinder our eyesight. We must ask God to open our eyes so we can see what he has in store for us. Hagar sees the well of water at the lowest moment in her life. She had more than enough water for her and Ishmael. In the middle of our wilderness, God provides a table. Now she could fill the empty bottle and heal her son. What a wonderful feeling that must have been.

SINGLE PARENTS-HAGAR – Being a single Mom is not an easy job but when it is just you and no one else, what do you do? Being a single Mom was extremely hard and sometimes hurtful. I had my parents while I was at school and my aunt helped, but after school, it was my son and myself. I had homework and other things to do, and it made for a long day. Unlike Hagar, her struggle was real, and she was all alone to raise her son. She had a promise and her son, and that is what she had to remember. I had a promise and my son, and I had to push.

Too many individuals are single parents because of unwanted circumstances, or because one parent leaves. Some people have children outside of marriage and face challenges, while others become single parents because of the death of a spouse. In my case, the dad decided that this was not his child and left. He has broken himself and we both were too young to have a child anyway, but it happened.

Like me, so many single parents found that new sense of courage and an additional source of strength that gave them the determination to move forward. But those who wait for the Lord shall renew their strength; They shall mount up with wings like eagles, they shall run and not be weary, they shall walk and not faint. Isaiah 40:31.

BLENDED FAMILIES – Now confront greater challenges than single-parent families, especially when it comes to disciplining children and helping them adjust to household rules and respect the stepparent. This puts a strain on families and sometimes hurts them. Many times, the stepchild is the cause of contention. Abraham had a choice to make regarding Hagar and Sarah. Many parents give up their children to please their spouse or family. This is very hurtful to the child and causes lots of hurt and anxiety to the family. With Abraham and Hagar's situation, God intervened and gave Abraham complete instructions on what to do. It's tough leaving behind a child you've brought into this world. It happened to me, and I suffered daily because of that decision. The emptiness in my life was hurtful, making me feel like my family was not complete. It's easier for men to leave their child, but as a woman, I can't because I went through the pain of carrying and delivering the child. God had a plan and purpose for us all, and I see it now. I loved my son unconditionally, and he was my blessing regardless of the circumstances or my situation.

The Lord's help can bring hope to every situation, and He can put back together those broken pieces.

Blended families are becoming increasingly popular. It is one of the greatest challenges of the new millennium. The church is falling behind in this ministry and lacks understanding of blended families, making the churches slow to provide help. Because of this, Satan is having his way with our families and generations of people. This child becomes discouraged, disillusioned, and distracted from the Kingdom of God. Satan's line of attacks has always been against the home and therefore we cannot give him any victory in our families.

My children who are married all have blended families as we all did. We raised the children with love and taught them to care for each other. Some of them even helped in daycare, and we also provided a temporary home for foster children. This can be a true ministry for the Lord.

CHAPTER 6

HANNAH'S BITTER SOUL

We can find the story of Hannah in *1 Samuel 1 and 2*. Her husband loved her, and everyone knew it except Hannah. She was going through it because her womb was closed. Being childless, she made a vow to God that if He would bless her with a son, she would give him back to the Lord all the days of his life.

But every year she would go with her husband worshipping and sacrificing to God in a place called Shiloh and every year the other wife (another woman) would show up. I could not imagine being in the same room with my husband's ex-girlfriend, much less a wife. But there she was, and so was Hannah. Her name was Peninnah, she was Elkanah's other wife. She was the wife that gave him lots of children. She was very fertile and was glad to let Hannah know it. Can you imagine yearly going up to worship and here comes the other wife pregnant again, and this was not just this time, but it was yearly? But Hannah got the double portion from Elkanah. She got most of the portions. Think about it like being child support and he would give Peninnah enough for the kids, but Hannah got the entire paycheck. He loved her more and he would express that to her. She just could not receive it because of her resentment.

Whenever Peninnah was around Hannah, she would purposely upset her by bringing up her infertility, making Hannah's life very difficult.

Is not that how the other woman does it? She provokes the actual wife to think that she has it all and makes her feel like she is nothing. Peninnah did it up. In my ministry, many women are separated from their husbands because of another woman and her family. They walk in pain and hurt as Hannah did, and that hurt turned to anger and from anger, resentment and now bitterness. Hannah was at that point as well. She was hurting and in pain but did not realize that she had the double portion. She had her husband's attention, but insecurity crept in, and all Hannah focused on was what Peninnah had and was giving Elkanah and what she could not. Hannah was thirsty.

Hannah was barren because God had prevented her from becoming pregnant. That was a prevailing diagnosis. She had an issue with being barren and the other woman kept conceiving children year after year.

The issue was spiritual, not physical. It was because God had refused to allow her to give birth. Hannah desperately desired a child, and this put her in bitterness of soul. Sometimes we can go through the pain, and it can become too familiar. Change does not come easy, and habits are hard to break, especially if you want to cause pain to another. So many women tolerate it in their lives. These women have come to kill, steal, and destroy. There have been so many women who have experienced something like Hannah. Barren, broken, bitter, and the other woman with an adversary.

To make matters worse, that woman taunted her about her barrenness, which grieved her deeply. She knew Hannah was his love, but her insecurities moved her. Have you ever been in a relationship where you were constantly in conflict with someone? Whether it's a coworker, neighbor, church member, or family member, there could be someone who consistently directs negativity toward you. Sometimes we find ourselves faced with people like that and like Peninnah, they enjoy relentless attacks on others. She teased her endlessly. This happens when we lose our focus and take it off God.

So, therefore, the provoking never stopped. Because hurt people hurt others and it hurt Peninnah because she did not receive the love that Hannah did from their husband. The difference between her and Hannah was that she could have babies as Hannah could not.

God wants to bless us and there are times we often get in the way. Sometimes women are jealous and love to provoke one another and hate to see others give birth to their vision. They do not want you to win or support the birth of your baby.

We sometimes have people on our jobs like that just torturing and teasing us so we can abort those dreams and purposes God has for us. Sometimes, there is a reason for putting them there. We may not understand why, but God knows all things. You have got to do what you need to do, and we should support one another.

Hannah took it to God. She had no more tears to cry, and the pain was too bad. It was taking her focus on her God and the prayer she prayed. If she held onto bitterness and lacked forgiveness, she would not receive communication from God, *Psalms 66:18*. She prayed openly and focused on God and not the adversary. She says, "My heart exalts in the Lord, my mouth speaks boldly against my enemies. Because I rejoice in your salvation, *1Samuel 2:1-2*. With deep distress, she offered a sincere prayer and wept bitterly, *1 Samuel 1:10*. She had a bitter soul. Without stopping, she prayed, fully committed to PUSH (Praying Until Something Happens). Her feelings towards the other woman and her children were genuine. She would not let go until she got blessed. As for Hannah, she was speaking and only moving her lips. She was speaking fervently from her heart. But her voice was not heard.

Though her husband believed she was intoxicated, she insisted that she was a woman with a sorrowful spirit and had not consumed any alcoholic beverages. Like some of us, we must focus on the blessing and our double portion and lay before the Lord until He moves. Hannah poured her heart out to the Lord. Her thirst was for changes in her life. She poured out all her hurts, pain, resentment, and bitterness, and repented to the Lord.

In her desire for God's attention, she disregarded the other woman and her kids. She was determined to have her prayers answered and not experience another barren day. The Lord answered, and she named her son Samuel. His name means "asked of God". She made that vow to God and kept it. She realized that her strength came from God and not from herself. Hannah endured mockery from Peninnah, was rebuked by her husband, and found solace in being heard by God. She was thirsty. But she knew God would quench her thirst. He was preparing her for something greater.

Sometimes we must get into our secret closet and pray. Set those healthy boundaries and block everything else out. Healthy boundaries help define identities, roles, and relationships. These boundaries pertain to our behavior and necessitate self-honesty. We must look that situation in the eye and recognize how we allow people to take control of us and take control of our interactions. And our unhealthy boundaries lead us to frustration, insecurity, resentment, and distrust. Making healthy boundaries can render positive results, but as you see, they do not come naturally. Hannah needed to get alone with God and allow Him to heal her everywhere she was hurting and mend her broken heart. All she has to do is surrender her secrets to God and submit herself to him. I poured out my heart to God and he listened to my cry.

Our hearts are filled with desires that often bring grief and pain, but God understands them. As time passes, Hannah realizes that God knows her story from start to finish and that everything has a purpose and a specific time. Accepting that season can be hard to navigate.

CHAPTER 7

POTIPHER'S DECEITFUL WIFE

Proverbs 22:14 (NIV) - The mouth of an adulterous woman is a deep pit; a man who is under the Lord's wrath falls into it.

Sometimes we believe we've achieved it all and are on top. Then something occurs in our lives that takes a downward spiral. We're all familiar with the tale of Joseph and his envious brothers, and the colorful coat bestowed upon him by his father. Their dysfunctional family dynamics led to Joseph being thrown into a pit and left for dead out of jealousy and hatred. Loved dearly by his father and hated by his brothers who sold him into slavery. He then became a slave to a foreign country. A slave owned by Potiphar, Joseph proves himself to Potiphar and now oversees Potiphar's entire estate. His conduct would lead him to lead his master to make him overseer of all he owned. Look at Joseph, favor. His life was about to change for the greater.

As overseer of Potiphar's house, Joseph would be over all the duties in his house and conduct important business for his master. Potiphar's household prospers because of Joseph.

PROSPERITY DOES NOT LEAD TO INTERNAL FULFILLMENT –Potiphar's wife had her every need provided for. She and her husband were wealthy and had a prominent position in Egypt as the captain of Pharaoh's bodyguard. Not only were they free from financial worries, but Joseph also blessed them.

Potiphar, an officer of Pharaoh, would often be away from home, leaving his wife alone with the young and handsome Hebrew slave. She craved that physical touch; she was "Thirsty" for it. Seeking affirmation and love, not wanting to feel alone. She had everything, but her husband was the only thing she needed. We do not know if her husband ignored her when he was home, caught up in his business, or if she was lonely and bored. All we know is that she was simply promiscuous and just needed someone to fulfill her sexual needs. She tries to seduce him. She would not stop, and she would do this day after day. Joseph refused her. One day, he came into the house to handle some business for Potiphar, and that is when she felt thirsty. She became aggressive, and physically grabbed him and tried to draw him towards her. He pulled away from her and leaving his jacket in her hands as he ran.

The scripture lets us know to stay away from evil women. Some are greedy, not submissive, rebellious, broken, wicked, adulterous, slandering, gossiping, and sexually immoral. Many have led great men to their downfall. Certain women with malicious intent try to make Christian men compromise and sin, and a few do give in. Numerous individuals have harmed their personal and professional lives by chasing a brief moment of sexual satisfaction.

Failing to get her thirsty desires met, her lust turns into rage. Calling her servants, she spreads false accusations about Joseph, alleging that he made inappropriate advances towards her. When she screamed for help, he ran away, leaving his coat behind. That was the evidence she relied on to back up her lie about him being in the house. When Potiphar comes back, she continues her lies and he instantly throws Joseph into prison without asking questions.

Proverbs 5:6-7 (NIV) - She gives no thought to the way of life; her paths wander, but she does not know it.

Proverbs 22:14 (NIV) - The mouth of an adulterous woman is a deep pit a man who is under the Lord's wrath falls into it.

Joseph is once again punished for something he didn't do. No one would believe the word of a slave, even though he was innocent of the adultery charges. Yet, they trusted the unfaithful spouse. He was not merely a slave, but also a prisoner in a foreign country. He was alone. With no family, friends, or hope of release, he felt trapped in prison. Joseph's only possession was his faith in God. He remained unchanged in prison. Throughout his entire life, he consistently behaved in a kind, obedient, honest, and trustworthy manner. When faced with adversity, this is how God wants us to be. He wants us to find joy in our trials, trust him, and remain steadfast.

Potiphar's wife was an unfaithful and lying spouse. She was a woman with no morals, unapologetic about her sexual cravings. Her lack of fulfillment made her vulnerable to temptation, always seeking to meet her fleshly needs. Whenever she felt unhappy or thirsty for fulfillment, she gravitated towards what she thought would do the trick. Her lack of intimacy or sexual fulfillment caused her to go down that road. Money was not a problem for her, but the wrong things enticed her.

Like Potiphar's wife, when people feel unfulfilled, they often fall into temptation. We witness this often in movies and the lives of movie stars and professionals. The common belief is that money solves everything, but it only provides material possessions, not true fulfillment. In marriage, it's important to have fulfillment and a mutual understanding of each other's love language.

Potiphar's wife had everything but the attention she needed from her husband. It's easy to get consumed by work or personal interests and neglect others. Our marriages become vulnerable because of a lack of sexual, emotional, and relational fulfillment. If your spouse is feeling thirsty and unfulfilled, there's a void that must be addressed. She needed to inform her husband about her unfulfilled desires, which intensified when he was away for long periods. So, she looked at Joseph with a fervent desire. She propositioned him daily and tempted him more and had it all planned so that her desires could be fulfilled. She had to tell her husband about her unsatisfied desires that grew when he was away. With fervent desire, she locked eyes with Joseph.

James: 1:14-15 (NLT) – Temptation comes from our desires, which entice and drag us away. These desires give birth to sinful actions. And when sin can grow, it gives birth to death.

Choices – *We* make choices because life is full of them. As we see, Potiphar's wife made an awful choice and because of her choices, it caused an innocent man to go to prison. All she wanted was to quench her thirst and move on. God will make things work out well for Joseph, despite Satan's evil plans. Potiphar's wife will have to face the consequences of her falsehood. Once you tell a lie, you have to keep up with it until it inevitably catches up to you. The things concealed in darkness will be revealed in the light. I'm confident she didn't get away with it because she had to face the consequences of her choices in her marriage. She remained responsible for the lies she told her husband.

CHAPTER 8

DELILAH'S DECEPTION

For the love of money is the root of all kinds of evil. Some people, eager for money, have wandered from the faith and pierced themselves with many griefs. (1 Timothy 6:10 NIV).

When we chase the promises of wealth, we find ourselves headed down the wrong trail and a path of betrayal. *Judges 16:4-5,* When we read Judges, we see there was an enormous amount of money that was offered to Delilah. It was exactly 5,500 pieces of silver and a fortune. Keep in mind, Delilah was a harlot, and it's probable that she worked for money, so this wouldn't have been strange to her. Being a Philistine, she was aware of Samson's actions against her people, throughout the story. Samson clearly has deep feelings for Delilah, but we don't know how she feels. She had the wrong motives and was solely working for money. This could be her ticket out of that life and provide lifelong care for her. Money itself doesn't cause betrayal, but being greedy for it does.

The desire for wealth, by any means necessary, is undeniable. Lust, not wealth, can lead us astray. Our desire for wealth might hinder our clarity and divert us from our goals. This would be a way out of that life for her and it would take care of her for the rest of her life. It is not money that causes us to walk down the path of betrayal, but it is the lust of it. It is the desire to be wealthy and by any means necessary. We do not have to have wealth to take us that way or lead us down the wrong path, but it is the lust. The desire to be wealthy could cloud our visions and make us fall from our purpose.

The pursuit of money can lead us to neglect our family and personal life. Money will cause people to lie and cheat on a business deal and even on government taxes. All these violations cause us to lose our values.

GIVE ME YOUR SECRET – All Delilah wanted to know was Samson's secret. She asked many times, and he lied many times, and eventually she realized that he never became vulnerable. She guilted Samson by questioning why he said "I love you" but didn't want to share his secret. Her plan was to manipulate Samson into confessing. Her talent lay in taming people through the art of manipulation and seduction. Using guilt to manipulate a loved one can ruin a relationship and erode trust.

HER ASSIGNMENT – Delilah can be that woman who sits in the pew in your church or at the desk on your job. Her assignment was to destroy men of prominence. She is the one who is broken and waiting on her next prey. She is a harlot, which is known as a modern-day gold digger, immoral and filled with ungodly and perverse sensual desires.

She is very creative and knows how to manipulate people to weaken the Body of Christ, regardless of their marital status. She is driven by money, manipulation, and control, which makes her vicious. Most deceptively, she will also appear to love God and deeply want you to think she cares about the salvation of souls. Delilah does not care if you are married. Her intentions are to kill, steal, and destroy. She's the woman who is always there to lend a shoulder and listen to your secrets. She actively works to ruin homes, marriages, and relationships. The skill of Delilah's spirit lies in seducing both men and women. Her mission is to gain power, make you weaker, and control you by using your secrets and weaknesses. She's so likable, she'll totally leave you puzzled, trying to figure her out. She is the one who leads the choir, the youth, and ushering at the door. I was often told to watch the tambourine player. She plays the tambourine, shouts, dances, and works her deceit. She's a master at manipulation and using people to divide the Body of Christ, regardless of their relationship status. She is vicious and money moves her as well as manipulation or control. Most deceptively, she will also appear to love God and deeply want you to think she cares about the salvation of souls. Delilah doesn't care about your marital status; she's here to wreak havoc. She's the kind of woman who's always there for you, ready to listen to all your secrets and comfort you. Her goal is to dismantle homes, marriages, and relationships. Her assignment is to use your weaknesses and secrets against you, imprisoning you and taking away your strengths.

Her physical armor comprises getting all dolled up, with her hair beautifully fixed and her clothes and shoes tight and appealing, all to target a man. She specifically targets individuals of prominence and uniqueness, including ministers, leaders, and people in the spotlight, and in ineffective relationships.

Delilah's intention in her relationship with Samson was to uncover his weakness, discover his secret, and report it to the Philistines. She cradled his head in her lap, skillfully manipulating him and ultimately breaking the strongest man in the world. She exposed his secret, leading to his downfall because of his vulnerability. Samson's lover betrayed him and caused him to lose his strength when she cut his hair, all because he disobeyed his vow. The source of his strength was the Spirit of God, and his hair served as a reminder that his strength was divine.

CHAPTER 9

BENT OUT OF SHAPE – A SPIRIT OF INFIRMITY

When Jesus saw her, he called her forward and told her, "Woman, I have set you free from your infirmity." Then he put his hands on her, and immediately she straightened up and praised God. *Luke 13:10-17.* Infirmity is a physical weakness and uncertainty that comes in many forms. It can result in depression, disappointment, low self-esteem, child abuse, and other issues. Can you imagine being bent over for eighteen years when you could not help yourself? Her situation did not just begin. It may have started in her childhood. These struggles were deep inside her and tainted many areas of her life.

***Bent Out of Shape** – I* had an attitude that caused me to be bitter, angry, and resentful. I experienced pain caused by someone else. It kept me from being free and walking in my greatness. My anger was so intense that I couldn't bear to hear that person's name. I was bitter, and that took me to another place. I walked in a darkness that was later diagnosed as depression. Here I am, a wife and mother, and could not be free. Being surrounded by negative words from people who were supposed to love me hindered and hurt me. This woman without a name struggled as well and, like her, I was struggling with my own emotional pain that kept my attitude wrong. What I did not understand, is that my attitude would hold a key to my deliverance and healing. I had to let go, and I had to forgive. Because I was hurting from all the childhood traumas, forgiveness is what would set me free.

Many others are crippled in the same way in their finances, emotions, and pain but Jesus wants us to empty all our trauma and pain on Him. *1 Peter 5:7* – Cast your cares on me because he cared for me. Jesus spoke to this nameless woman's spirit; he spoke to her pain and her emotions. He called her 'Woman" and that meant a lot to her. God says in *Psalms 139:14* that – *we are fearfully and wonderfully made, and His works are marvelous.* You see, God does not make junk and we should allow no one to speak into our lives negatively. We should be resilient like the woman with blood, pushing forward regardless of others' opinions. We need to have faith in the process and let God address the pain within us. Trust in the Lord with all thine heart and lean not into your own understanding, (*Proverbs 3:5 - KJV*). The enemy worked against her until she recognized she needed to break free. She had a choice and realized that she would either be this way always or she could straighten up her situation.

I spent half of my life bent out of shape in a pain that I did not need. Not realizing that resentment and bitterness caused my issues, I had to let them go. It was not easy because I had been carrying it around for over forty years or for as long as I could remember from childhood. That pain had me turn to a sinful life where I quieted the noise from the negative words that were said to me as I was growing up. A pain that kept me in quiet tears. I could not find peace anywhere, and especially not within.

Like this woman who was desperate for a miracle for eighteen years, so was I. You see that pain became too familiar. Ungodly relationships did as well. My attitude affected my freedom because I did not want to let go. I knew I needed it corrected, but how? One day, my husband taught a bible study about bitterness. It hit me where that pain was in my heart. I cried. God wants to free us from pain and bitterness so that we can let go of our negative attitude and move forward without being held back by pain. I had to learn that my attitude affected my situation and hindered my healing and all the things I desired for God to do in my life. What a blessing. Finally, I could be free. When God comes to heal, He heals emotions too. Just like the woman with the issue of blood. When he laid his hands on her, she instantly straightened up and praised God, *Luke 13:13.*

Her attitude changed, and so did mine. She began to leap and magnify God. Mentally, physically, and emotionally, I was restored. That root of bitterness was killing me and everything I worked for in life.

She broke free from those insecurities, as he called her out of her wounded, broken, hurtful situation and gave her a new attitude. He wants to release you from all the things Satan said you cannot have and cause you to stand in His strength.

God has a plan for you, and he recognizes the possibility of what you can become. He sees that you have potential. That is why he called me out. That is why he spoke to your spirit and began to release your dreams. Our pain is our story, and that suffering has made me into a different woman from the one He originally intended for me to be.

You can always trust God to be there for you, walk beside you, and be ready to walk you through situations you may face. You are never alone; He is greater than any problem we will face. He is faithful. When you need him, He will deliver you. He's waiting for you to call on him. Let it go and hear Him say, "Woman thou art Loosed for your infirmity."

CHAPTER 10

REHAB – FAITH FOR HER FAMILY

Rahab's story begins at an Inn where travelers or locals come for food and lodging. It may have been a place where strangers would come to enter and gain information without being noticed. Rahab had a business that may have kept the travelers busy. She was a harlot. Some would call her profession a prostitute. She was a sinful woman with a pagan background who recognized the God of Israel as being the one and only true God. Her affection for the Israelites and their God led her to abandon the God of the Canaanites. She heard about all the miracles in the wilderness, and it was hidden in her heart.

A group of spies visited Rehab's traveler's lodge seeking out the land and decided to stay there. One day, the king summoned Rahab to bring forth the men who were staying at her inn, but she hid them and lied instead. As far as her morals were concerned, Rahab possessed none. She did not adhere to any laws or covenants and did not even act as if she had any convictions. But God does not need to rely on deception to fulfill His covenant to protect those spies or anyone else. He was a God of truth and honesty. You shall know the truth and the truth will make you free.

Can you imagine one situation changing your life? It wasn't by accident that those spies showed up at Rahab's lodge. It was a divine appointment from God, whether or not she knew it. All she knew was that she lied and kept their stay there a secret. She knew she helped those spies escape and did not understand that it was a part of a plan God had already put in place. God uses those foolish things of life to confound the wise. God chose the spies to go to Rehab because he knew she would play a key role in the Israelite victory over Jericho. No matter who they are or what they've been through, God can use regular believers to fulfill His will.

Rehab's story may not have been mine, but I, too, am a sinner that God is using. God saw something in me and took me out of an old pit. He brought me into His marvelous light. Although I wasn't hiding spies, there were other things in my life I concealed due to pain and hurt. I was hiding bitterness for years. I was hiding my anger and resentment. God saw greatness, but I did not. He saw something that was promising, and I only saw defeat. I always looked out for others and helped others to escape from pain and hurt but, no one was there for me. While Rahab may have lied and there is no mention of any negativity surrounding her lie, I even knew that lying was a sin and yet I did it. So, she hid those spies on the rooftop, telling them that God had already given them the land; as well as how she heard the Lord dried up the Red Sea and brought them out of Egypt.

When hearing the word of God, I remember how it increased my faith as I saw what God could do. He brought me out of the wilderness and delivered me from that which was bitter and sometimes sweet. As a result, I chose not to go back to the place where I felt hurt and pain. Amid drugs, alcohol, and a party life that I thought would take me out of here without hope, he delivered me. He parted my Red Sea and brought me across on dry land to increase my faith. So, I had to make a choice to put my trust in the Lord. I had to trust that He would deliver me and my family from a life of intentional sin.

Now, therefore, I pray you, swear unto me by the Lord since I have shared your kindness that you will also shew me kindness unto my father's house and give me a true token: and that you save my Father, mothers, brother, sisters and all that they have and deliver our lives from death – Joshua 2:12-13 KJV.

I prayed a similar prayer, but now I pray for my deliverance and God saving my husband. Being saved as a young couple living in Livorno, Italy was difficult, especially after giving birth, because there were no friends for support, no place to worship, and my husband wasn't thinking about God. So, as the journey continued, I was obedient and continued to pray. Like Rahab, I recognized God as an all-powerful God. A God that could do anything but fail. He kept his promises.

Scarlet Ribbon – My scarlet ribbon was the word of God. *Joshua 1:7-9* I learned I had to be strong and obedient so that I could be successful. He would hear my cry and answer my prayer. *Jeremiah 29:11 – He knows the plans He had for me.* Confirmation for me was knowing that He would deliver my family if I remained obedient. God told Joshua that in order to succeed, we must obey the rules found in His word. I had to trust in Him with all my heart and not lean on my understanding. *Proverbs 3:5* It was also crucial for Rahab to hang out that scarlet ribbon and to keep everything quiet so as not to lose her family to the destruction of Jericho.

When we pray to hear from God, we must sometimes keep it to ourselves and tell no one what we are praying for. Often, we cannot see our future results, but if we trust God, we will see the great benefits He has planned for us. I had to set time aside daily to seek the Lord, read his word, and meditate on it day and night. Rahab had no choice but to obey God, since it would cost her family's salvation if she did not. I had to trust God for my family to be saved as well.

CHAPTER 11

GOMER – THE PREACHER'S UNFAITHFUL WIFE

Let the morning bring me word of your unfailing love. I have put my trust in you. Show me the way I should go, for to you I entrust my life. Psalms 143:8 (NIV).

Gomer in the book of Hosea was the unfaithful wife of Hosea the Prophet. God used Hosea and Gomer's relationship to show how Israel had sinned by worshiping idols, but His love never wavered. He is always faithful when we are not. God told Hosea to go marry a promiscuous woman and have children with her. Like an adulterous wife, this land is guilty of being unfaithful to God, *Hosea 1:2*. Hosea was obedient and married Gomer, and they had two sons and a daughter.

Many times, individuals do not have their emotional needs met during their childhood and approach marriage with a painful deficit of emotions, hoping their spouse will fulfill those needs for them. They enter a world of marriage unaccustomed to their spouses only to provide for them.

There is no evidence that Gomer went back to her old lifestyle after bearing three children, but we know she had an adulterous thirst, even with her ideal husband, Hosea.

Adultery is wrong, and God will judge the adulterer and all sexual immorality. It is important to commit the pain of being betrayed by the person who knows every detail of the situation and confront it appropriately when it happens. In the same way, being unfaithful brings emotional pain, and Christians should rely on God, who cares for them, *1Peter 5:7*. This marriage was God's way of showing God's people they were committing spiritual adultery. Only through repentance and seeking God can we avoid returning to our old lifestyle. First, getting saved and then moving to another country with no spiritual strength is a memory I can still recall. I didn't feel God's presence, and I didn't realize I went back to my old habits. However, as I put down the cigarettes and left the party, I picked up my old attitude. Despite my lack of understanding, God's unconditional love was always with me, even while I did not feel it. He heard my cries and dried my tears. As a storm raged through my life, he was my shelter, but I had no relationship with him like that to understand that truth.

God instructed Hosea to show love to his wife again, *Hosea 3:1*. Show her love as God loved the Israelites. Love her as it did not hurt. That is what Hosea did for Gomer, and that is what God did for me. This is just a reflection of what Jesus Christ does for us. His healing, restoration, forgiveness, and freedom are all available to us, and he paid the price one day for you and me. He died for us while we were still sinners. He covers all our sins and redeems us back to him. God's love is unfailing. His love is undying and who could love us like that but God?

CHAPTER 12

I'M THIRSTY – IT'S ALL IN THE RELATIONSHIP

But whosoever drink of this water that I shall give him shall never thirst again. John 4:14 (KJV).

Can you imagine Jesus coming to your town for a drink of water? He needed to quench his thirst because he was dehydrated. It was Noonday, extremely hot, and Jesus was tired from traveling. En route to Samaria, he stopped at Jacobs well outside a town called Sychar. The disciples went into town for food. So, he was there alone and just like Jesus, there will be times you will have to do it alone because people can be a hindrance to your calling.

When this nameless woman appeared at the well with a clay pot in her hand, Jesus used the opportunity to ask her for a drink, *John 4:7*. She was a nameless Samaritan woman at the well. An extraordinary woman, and the Jews had no dealings with her kind.

Historically, Jews were not allowed to communicate with Samaritans, especially women, unless their husbands were present.

The Samaritans, a mixed race of Jews and pagans, were completely despised by the Jewish community. It reminded me of the time when my sons were dating outside of their race. When they brought them to church, the youth pastor told them to stick with their kind. They did not draw them to God; they pushed them away because of their prejudiced attitudes towards mixed relationships.

That was hurtful and they all married women from other races and cultures and Jesus is not holding it against them as he did not towards this woman. That was the reason she came to the well in the heat of the day. She wanted to avoid other women who shamed her or scorned her for her lifestyle as a prostitute who was married multiple times.

What made it even worse was she was shacking up with a man and not married. In any race, that is an abomination. Instead of being looked down on or being called names, she avoided the embarrassment by choosing to get water in the heat of the day. She had a past, a pain, and an emptiness. She was lost and caught up in the search for her direction. Many problems arose because of her isolation that she had to confront.

Let us consider the issues she faced:

1. Her race, because she was a Samaritan, and scorned by the Jews (like African Americans in the USA during the pre-civil rights era and even today).
2. She was confused and disheartened.
3. She had no rights as a woman in her culture.
4. She was married and divorced five times.
5. She was living with a man that she was not married to.
6. Five times she attempted to find someone who could satisfy her thirst but was unsuccessful.
7. She suffered from low self-esteem because of the way others viewed her.

During their encounter at the well, Jesus questioned her and she honestly expressed her truths. She was a woman burdened by pain, haunted by her past, and shunned by many because of her background. Seeking love, she made numerous attempts, yet found no success. The internal struggle she faced didn't occur suddenly but developed gradually through multiple relationships.

The Bible didn't clarify if she had been in abusive relationships and the reasons behind her numerous divorces were unclear. Yet, countless women battle with infirmities caused by emotional traumas and lack the knowledge to overcome the pain. The people in her neighborhood tormented her because she was different from them and suffered racial discrimination. A marriage would not be enough to relieve her pain, so she decided to live with a man instead until one day she met Jesus. He knew her and wanted her to share her truth. She needed Jesus to heal her pain, so he let her know he had water that would quench her thirst and she would never be thirsty again. He began to speak life, deliverance, and restoration over her. Jesus explained to her how she could recover the things she had lost, and how she could break free of all those entanglements. It was up to her to allow Jesus to touch all the places where she was hurting.

Her Choices – No matter who we are, we all have made choices in our lives. *James 4:7* tells us to submit, therefore, unto God and resist the devil and he will flee from us. There are times when we need to submit and resist and allow God to take charge of our lives. Change our mindset and direction and fight against those entanglements. To quench her thirst, Jesus confessed the truth about his water. *Everyone who drinks this well water will be thirsty again (John 4:13 - NIV), but whoever drinks the water I give him will never thirst.*

Jesus shifted her everyday life to everlasting life by allowing her to see the value of this living water. Her failed relationships didn't matter anymore. Her regrets didn't matter anymore. She could now be free from emptiness and loneliness and find her inner beauty and purpose. It is easy to lose sight of our spiritual needs when we focus on satisfying our physical desires. So, when we see something new, we become thirsty for it. We are destroyed by our lack of knowledge and understanding, *Hosea 4:6.*

Speaking the Truth in Love – After hearing Jesus' request to get her husband and return, she hesitated and then sighs, "I don't have a husband." He wanted to know her truth and hopes she would tell him. He affirmed her answer and exposed her sin. Jesus said *you told the truth; in fact, you have five husbands and the one you are living with is not your husband. (John 4:18).*

Despite making many mistakes in our lives and being bashed down and judged by them, we want to block them out. We want to leave that part out of our discussion. Divorce is not something we want to talk about, especially five divorces. The woman at the well was broken and in sin. There was a void in her life. She was thirsty, and she needed deliverance. She realized Jesus was a prophet who knew things only she knew. Her secrets were out. Only God could provide the deliverance she needed for her problem. She needed love, but first, she needed to love herself. She drank this water Jesus told her about and went to tell everyone else about the man who changed her life. Her shame left her. Her sins were forgiven, and her past was her past. She could now break free.

Once you recognize who Jesus is in your life, you can call out to him and lift your hands in praise, running to tell everybody what he has done for you. Regardless of your past or current sins, there is a distinction between being saved and being healed. Salvation is deliverance and can happen instantly, but healing is a process. In each of us, there is something that needs to be healed, and until it heals, we are weak and can fall back into sin. Even though your spirit is saved, there may be areas in your mind, heart, emotions, and desires that require healing. Allow God into that secret place because wholeness comes when you do. Turn all your weaknesses over to him. Give him your pain, hurt, and all your concerns. Break free from those struggles and shame. He is the only prescription for any problem you may have. Give it to Him. All of it. And never thirst again. You may not change the past, but you, sure enough, can change your future. God restores, delivers, and sets the captive free.

Choices and Consequences – We make choices multiple times a day. Some of our choices are small and some shape the course of our lives. In Eve's case, we see the choice she made when she faced the enemy. That choice changed her life and that of her entire family. Her choice came with great punishment, and it affects us all today. Eve lost much more. Because of her choice, she became homeless, and they had to immediately leave the garden and start all over. Her family was dysfunctional, and Adam had to get a job where the labor was hard. You see Eve was the first wife, mother, and the first mom to lose two sons, one to death and another one to wandering in a land he did not know where he was. This place was called Nod.

Now Sarah fell off her faith and followed her mind. She took matters into her own hands, and, like Eve, she heard God, but it was easy to do it her way. Losing her faith made her think about her age. She thought she was too old to give birth to her promise. She did not understand that with God, all things are possible. *Matthew 19:26.* She laughed, and God told her He would be back at that appointed time. So, you see, we all have that appointed time for our blessing, our dream, and our purpose, but we must trust God and quiet all the noise. Well, Sarah talked her husband into falling into a trap and knew good and well what God had spoken to her about the appointed time. We must realize the appointed time with God will lead to the promise He has for us. To everything, there is a season and a time under the sun. *Ecclesiastes 3:1* We must be patient and understand God's timing is not ours and He will come through.

In life, we are all thirsty for the wrong things and, at some point, suffer the consequences of our actions. Sometimes our punishment is greater than the choice, but it is because we did not follow the instructions that God has set before us. *Proverbs 3:5-6* says to trust Him with all our hearts and acknowledge him in all thy ways and He will direct our paths.

My parents warned us about the type of company we keep and taught us about getting in the wrong crowds or starting off on the wrong track. And guess what we did? We did it our way and found the hard way. I was told that I would be nothing or go nowhere in my life because I was angry all the time. Well, I set out to prove them wrong and found myself spending time with the wrong crowd, in the streets, and partying, all while having a child at home who was depending on me. It was the hurt that triggered the bad choices I made and the pain that pushed me into many things I cannot even explain. All I knew was that I had a praying grandmother who never stopped praying for me.

The choices I made hurt really bad in the end, and I realized how my thirst of looking for others to love me and things to console me was even more hurtful. A choice is instant, but the pain of poor choices lingers on until we are healed. Otherwise, you remain empty, broken, and bent over. Can you imagine twelve years of hurt/pain, low self-esteem, anxiety, depression, and much more weighing you down?

No one understands because they think after you get saved, it should all go away. Like the woman in *Luke 13 where Jesus* touched her and said, *Woman Thou Art Loosed,* and immediately, she was made whole. It's not that simple. The woman with the issue needed to touch God, and He spoke into her life. So, at that moment, her situation dried up. Deliverance is not prejudice and anyone can experience the need no matter what level of faith they may have. Sometimes you must push through the crowds, turn off the noise from the crowd, and reach for your promise. In this case, her promise was healing. She did not care about what anyone said or about her situation. She remained focused and pushed herself free.

Then there are women like Leah. Very pretty, who hide in relationships where they are not loved, but used for sexual needs. Confusing love with lust and not realizing all he wants is a one-night stand. Leah had hoped, but his heart was with another woman. The woman he loved was her sister. Can you imagine being compared to another? Being hated by them both, but still making herself available to him. Eventually, Leah would choose to break free. She pushed through her pain to break free from Jacob. It was necessary for her to find her own path and understand that life had more to offer than being someone's romantic interest. She realized she had choices, and the choice was to break free or stay in the pain.

Some women have a tough time breaking from sexual soul ties and it keeps them bound in relationships where they cannot move forward. Leah realized God gave her a gift of purpose, and it was time for her to walk in it.

Our Choices – We all have the same gift of purpose, and we will always face choices. Like the woman with the infirmity for eighteen years of being broken, bent over, having issues, and thirsty for many relationships. God spoke to her and each of the women mentioned in this book, and we witnessed the impossible become possible. All they needed was someone to speak life into their situation. They were all thirsty but needed a *Renewed Thirst,* including me, to be whole again. God's promises never return void and when we seek Him, he hears and acts on his promises. Now, GO and gain a *Renewed Thirst,* and watch God turn it around for your good.

ABOUT THE AUTHOR

Lorraine Jones-Whitfield is the wife of Elder Carlton Whitfield Sr. Her mission is to assist people in living by God's word and fulfilling their purpose. Her expertise is in Marriage and Family, Children's Ministry, Christian Life Coaching, and Mental Health Coaching. She is the CEO of Hannah's Heart Ministry and S.H.E. Soars LLC. She supports women through online book ministry, family and marriage ministry, and mentoring. Her mission also includes providing resources and services like Women's Prayer Breakfast and empowerment sessions, as well as her AIT Boot Camps for personal development where they W.I.N. (Walk in Newness). She is also available to speak at women's events.

She and her husband, Elder Carlton, have seven children and fourteen grandchildren. They have been married for over forty three years and live in Wilson, North Carolina. They are involved in ministry and run a successful marriage and family counseling group.

Her social media connections are:

Website: https://www.shesoarsfaith.com
Facebook: https://www.facebook.com/lorraine.Whitfield
Email: shespeakslife7@gmail.com

Made in the USA
Middletown, DE
15 October 2024